Alchemy in the Nineteenth Century

By Helena P. Blavatsky

Copyright © 2020 Lamp of Trismegistus. All rights reserved. No part of this publication may be reproduced or transmitted in any form or by any means, electronic or mechanical, including photocopying, recording, or by any information storage and retrieval system, without permission in writing from Lamp of Trismegistus. Reviewers may quote brief passages.

ISBN: 978-1-63118-446-8

Esoteric Classics

Other Books in this Series and Related Titles

Magical Essays and Instructions by Florence Farr (978-1-63118-418-5)

Ancient Mysteries and Secret Societies by Manly P. Hall (978-1-63118-410-9)

Lost Atlantis and the Gods of Antiquity & Plato's History of Atlantis by Carolus Kiesewetterus & Manly P. Hall (978-1-63118-431-4)

The Human Aura: Astral Colors and Thought Forms by Swami Panchadasi and William Walker Atkinson (978-1-63118-419-2)

Ancient Egyptian Mysteries and Hieroglyphics, Modern Freemasonry & Initiation of the Pyramid by various authors (978-1-63118-430-7)

Essays on the Esoteric Tradition of Karma by William Q. Judge, Helena P. Blavatsky & Annie Besant (978-1-63118-426-0)

The Secrets of Enoch by Enoch (978-1-63118-449-9)

The Smoky God or A Voyage to the Inner World by Willis George Emerson (978-1-63118-423-9)

The Gospel of the Nativity of Mary by St. Matthew (978-1-63118-448-2)

The Mysteries of Freemasonry & the Druids by Albert G. Mackey, Manly P. Hall, &c (978-1-63118-444-4)

History, Analysis and Secret Tradition of the Tarot by Manly P. Hall, A. E. Waite &c (978-1-63118-445-1)

Rosa Alchemica, The Tables of Law & The Adoration of the Magi by William Butler Yeats (978-1-63118-421-5)

Audio Versions are also Available on Audible and iTunes

Table of Contents

Introduction…7

Part I: Prologue…9

Alchemy in the Nineteenth Century…11

Introduction

The word "esoteric" can be difficult to define. Esotericism in general can be seen less as a system of beliefs and more as a category, which encompasses numerous, different systems of beliefs. It's a bit of juxtaposition, since the word "esoteric" indicates something that few people know about, while the term itself broadly covers numerous philosophies, practices, areas of study and belief systems.

In a greater sense, Esotericism acts as a storehouse for secret knowledge, which is often considered ancient (by *tradition, if not by fact*), passed down from generation to generation, in private. At various times in history, simply possessing the knowledge of some of these subjects, was considered illegal and a jailable offence, if discovered. This usually included such general topics as Alchemy, Qabalah, Hermeticism, Occultism, Ceremonial Magic, Astrology, Divination, Rosicrucianism and so on. Collectively, these areas of study were often referred to as the esoteric sciences.

Sometimes, the outer garment of a subject isn't esoteric, while what is hidden beneath it, is. As an example, Freemasonry isn't necessarily esoteric by nature (at *least not anymore*), but certain signs, passwords and handshakes given to the candidate during their initiation, are in fact, esoteric, in the sense that they are hidden from the general public.

Today, in the twenty-first century, such topics are readily available at bookstores across the country, and numerous mainsteam publishers offer beginners guides and coffee-table volumes on many of these subjects, intended for mass appeal. Books like *"The Secret"* have turned previously arcane topics into household knowledge. All that being the case, however, it isn't to say that there still aren't buried secrets to uncover, ancient wisdom being ignored and forgotten mysteries to be explored. In fact, it is often that we are only able to further our own studies by standing on the shoulders of these disappearing giants.

Lamp of Trismegistus is doing its part to help preserve humanity's esoteric history by making some of these classics available to those students who are seeking to unearth the knowledge of these ancient colossi.

So, be sure to check other titles from our *Esoteric Classics* series, as well as our *Occult Fiction, Theosophical Classics, Foundations of Freemasonry* and our *Christian Apocrypha Series.* You can also download the audio versions of most of these titles from iTunes or Audible, for learning on the go.

Preface

Oral tradition dates the discovery of alchemy to over 5,000 years ago, in Egypt. While we often think of it as largely European, traces of it being written about and practiced, exist far beyond a single country or continent.

The place of alchemy in history is often viewed as sordid and fantastical. In the minds of many, it conjures up images of foolish men in dungeon laboratories, using archaic apparatus to transmute lead into gold. Without a doubt, the alchemical literature of the sixteenth and seventeenth centuries did contain ongoing references to such a process; however, with most alchemical manuscripts having been thickly written in symbolic language and allegory, many scholars contend that it wasn't physical gold that the alchemists were after, but spiritual gold, resulting from the transformation of the spirit of the individual. This is often referred to as "internal alchemy," and it is a popular explanation for twenty-first century citizens to accept. In spite of this seemingly reasonable interpretation, it can be difficult to overlook the detailed procedures and instructions, which are often contained in many of the manuscripts, descriptions which, even the most creative minds would have difficulty arguing are instructions intended for spiritual liberation.

One thing that is inarguable, however, is that alchemy was an important step in the development of modern chemistry and medicine. Due to their valuable contributions, Renaissance era alchemists such as Paracelsus and Isaac Newton have secured themselves a place in mainstream history books, in spite of their predilection toward what is now considered pseudoscience.

Alchemy in the Nineteenth Century

By Helena P. Blavatsky

The language of archaic chemistry or Alchemy has always been, like that of the earlier religions, symbolical.

We have shown in the *Secret Doctrine* that everything in this world of effects has three attributes or the triple synthesis of the seven principles. In order to state this more clearly, let us say that everything which exists in the world around us is made up of three principles and four aspects just as we have shown to be the case with man.

As man is a complex unity consisting of a body, a rational soul and an immortal spirit so each object in nature possesses an objective exterior, a vital soul, and a divine spark which is purely spiritual and subjective.

The first of this threefold proposition cannot be denied, the second cannot logically be objected to, for if we admit that metals, certain woods, minerals and drugs possess inherent powers to produce effects on living organisms, then official science practically admits its truth. As for the third, of the presence of an absolute quintessence in each atom, materialism, which deals only with the *anima mundi,* denies it utterly.

Much good may it derive from this agnostic attitude. We for our part, finding in materialism an undoubted proof of the existence of moral and spiritual blindness, make no account of the denial and, leaving the blind to lead the blind, proceed with our subject.

Thus as with natural objects, so every science has its three fundamental principles and may be applied through all three or by the use of only one of them.

Before Alchemy existed as a science its quintessence alone acted in nature's correlations (as indeed it still does) and in all its planes.

When there appeared on earth men endowed with a superior intelligence they allowed this supreme power to have full and uncontrolled action and from it they learnt their first lessons. All that they had to do was to imitate it. But in order to reproduce the same effects by an effort of individual will, they were obliged to develop in their human constitution a power called Kriyasakti in occult phraseology.

This faculty is creative, and is so simply because it is the agent on an objective plane of the first creative principle. It resembles a lightning conductor in that it conducts and gives definite direction to the creative quintessence which otherwise, if led blindly into the lower planes, kills; but which brought down through the channel of the human intellect creates according to a predetermined plan.

From this Alchemy was born; and magnetic magic, and many other branches of the tree of occult science.

When in the course of ages nations grew up so intensely saturated with egotism and vanity as to be convinced of their complete superiority to all others living in the present, or who had lived in the past; when the development of Kriyasakti became more difficult and the divine faculty had almost disappeared from the earth, then they forgot little by little the wisdom of their ancestors. They even went further and rejected altogether the tradition of their antediluvian parents, denying with contempt the presence of a spirit and of a soul in this the most ancient of all sciences. Of the three great attributes of nature they only accepted the existence of matter or rather its illusory aspect, for of real matter or *substance* even the materialists themselves confess a complete ignorance; and truly they are right, nor have they even the vaguest conception of what it is.

Thus there grew up the science of modern chemistry.

Change is the constant effect of cyclic evolution. The perfect circle becomes One, a triangle, a quaternary and a quinary. The creative principle issued from the rootless root of absolute existence, which has neither beginning nor end, and of which the symbol is the serpent or *perpetuum mobile* swallowing its tail in order to reach its head, has become the Azoth of the alchemists of the middle ages. The circle becomes a triangle, emanating the one from the other as Minerva from the head of Jupiter. The circle hypothecates the absolute; the right line issuing from it represents a metaphysical synthesis and the left a physical one. When Mother Nature shall have made of her body a line joining these two, then will come the moment of awakening for the Cosmic Activity. Until then Purush, the spirit, is separated from Prakriti — material nature still unevolved. Its legs exist only in a state of potentiality, and cannot move nor has it arms wherewith to work on the objective forms of things sublunary. Wanting in limits, Purush cannot begin to build until it has mounted into the neck of Prakriti the blind, when the triangle will become the microcosmic star. Before reaching this stage they must both pass through the quaternary state and that of the cross which conceives, this is the cross of earthly mystics, who make a great display of this their beflowered symbol, namely: the cross divided into four parts, which may be read Taro, Ator, and Rota, Tora. The Virgin, or adamic earth substance which was the Holy Spirit of the old Alchemists of the Rosy Cross, has now been changed by the Kabbalists, those flunkeys to modern science, into Na^2Co^3 Kali and C^2H^6O or Alcohol.

Ah! Star of the morning, daughter of the dawn, how fallen from thine high estate — poor Alchemy. All on this ancient planet, thrice deceived, is doomed to tire and, sliding into oblivion, to be destroyed; and yet that which once was, is and shall be for ever, even to the end of time. Words change and the meaning underlying them becomes quickly disfigured. But the ideas which are their root and parent shall endure. The ass' skin in which nature's queen wrapped herself in order to deceive fools as in the story of Perrault — for the disciple of the old philosophers will always recognize the truth, no matter under what garb, and will adore it, this ass' skin we must believe is more congenial to the tastes of modern philosophy and materialistic alchemists, who sacrifice the living soul for the empty form, than Royal Nature naked and unadorned. And thus it is that the skin only falls before Prince Charming, who recognizes in the ring sent the marriage betrothal.

To all those courtiers who hover round Dame Nature while cutting at her material envelope, she has nothing to present but her outer skin. It is for this reason that they console themselves by giving new names to old things, old indeed as the world itself, declaring loudly the while that they have discovered something new. The necromancy of Moses has in this way become modern Spiritualism; and the Science of the old initiates of the temple, the magnetism of the gymnosophists of India; the healing mesmerism of Sculapius "the Savior," is only received now on condition that it is called hypnotism, in other words Black Magic under its proper title.

Modern materialists would have us believe that Alchemy or the transmutation of base metals into gold and silver has from the earliest ages been nothing more than charlatanism. According to them it is not a science but a superstition, and therefore all those who believe, or pretend to believe in it, are either dupes or impostors. Our encyclopedias are full of abusive epithets leveled at Alchemists and Occultists.

Now, gentlemen of the French Academie, this may be all very well, but if you are so sure of yourselves, let us have at least some clear and irrefutable proof of the absolute impossibility of the transmutations of metals. Tell us how it is that a metallic base is found even in alkalis. We know certain scientists, men of recognized ability even, who think that the idea of reducing the elements to their first state and even to their primordial essence is not so stupid as it seemed at first sight. Gentlemen, these elements when once you have admitted that they all existed in the beginning in one igneous mass, from which *you* say the earth's crust has been formed, these may be reduced again and brought through a series of transmutations to be once more that which they originally were. The question is to find a solvent sufficiently strong to effect in a few days or even years that which nature has taken ages to perform. Chemistry and, above all, Mr. Crookes has sufficiently proved that there exists a relationship between metals so marked as to indicate not only a common source but an identical genesis.

Then, Gentlemen, I would ask you who laugh at alchemy and alchemists with a mirth bred of a consciousness of superior wisdom, how it is that one of your first chemists, M. Berthold, author of *La Synthese,* deeply read in alchemical lore, is unable to deny to alchemists *a most profound knowledge of matter.*

And again, how is it that M. Chevreul, that venerable sage, whose great age, no less than his living to the last in the full possession of all his faculties, has moved to wonder our present generation, which, with its over-weening self-sufficiency, is so difficult to penetrate or rouse; how comes it, we say, that he who made so many practical and useful discoveries for modern industry, should have possessed so many works on alchemy.

Is it not possible that the key to his longevity may be found in one of these very works, which according to you is but a collection of superstitions as useless as they are ridiculous.

The fact remains that this great savant, the father of modern chemistry, took the trouble to bequeath after his death, to the library of the Museum, the numerous works he possessed on this "false science," and here in this act of his we have an unmistakable revelation of the estimation in which he held them. Nor have we yet heard that those luminaries of science attached to this sanctuary have thrown these books on alchemy into the waste paper basket as useless rubbish full of fantastic reveries engendered by the sick imagination of a diseased brain.

Besides, our wise men forget two things — in the first place never having found the key to these hermetic books, they have no right to decide whether this *jargon* preaches truth or falsehood, and secondly, that wisdom was certainly not born for the first time with them, nor must it necessarily disappear from the world on their demise.

Each science, we repeat, has its three aspects; all will grant that there must be two, the objective and the subjective. Under the first head we may put the alchemical transmutations with or without the powder or projection; under the second we place all speculations concerning the nature of the mind. Under the third is hidden a high and spiritual meaning. Now since the symbols of the two first are identical in design and possess moreover, as I have tried to prove in the *Secret Doctrine*, seven interpretations varying with their application to either of the three natural kingdoms the physical, the psychic, or the purely spiritual, it will be easily understood that only great initiates are able to correctly interpret the jargon of hermetic philosophers. And then again, since there exist more false than true hermetic writings, even those of Hermes himself may be found distorted. Who does not know for example, that a certain series of formulas may be correctly applied to the solving of concrete problems of technical alchemy while these same on being employed to render an idea belonging to the psychological plane will possess an entirely different meaning? Our late brother Kenneth Mackenzie expresses this well when he says, speaking of Hermetic Societies:

> For the practical alchemist whose object was the production of gold by the use of laws belonging especially to his own peculiar art, the evolution of a mystic philosophy was of secondary importance, for his work could be carried on without any direct reference to a system of theosophy, whilst the Sage who had raised himself to a superior plane of metaphysical contemplation rejected naturally the simply material part of his studies, finding it beneath his aspirations. —
> *Royal Masonic Cyclopaedia*

Thus it becomes evident that symbols taken as guides to the transmutation of metals, become of small value to those methods which we now call *chemical*. There is yet another question we would like to ask: — Who of our great men would dare to treat as impostors such men as Paracelsus, Van Helmont, Roger Bacon, Boerhaven and many other illustrious alchemists?

While French Academicians mock at the Kabbalah as well as at alchemy (*though at the same time taking from this latter their inspirations and their many discoveries*) the Kabbalists and occultists of Europe begin *sub rosa* to prosecute the Secret sciences of the East. In fact the wisdom of the Orient does not exist for our wise men of the West; it died with the Magi. Nevertheless, alchemy, which if we search diligently we shall find as the foundation of every occult science — comes to them from the far East. Some pretend that it is only the posthumous evolution of the magic of the Chaldeans. We shall try to prove that this latter is only the heir, first to an antediluvian alchemy, and then to an alchemy of the Egyptians. Olaus Borrichius, an authority on this question, tells us to search for its origin in the remotest antiquity.

To what epoch may we ascribe the origin of alchemy? No modern writer is able to tell us exactly. Some give us Adam as its first Adept; others place it to the account of an indiscretion of "the sons of God, who seeing that the daughters of man were beautiful, took them for their wives." Moses and Solomon are later Adepts in the science, for they were preceded by Abraham, who was in turn antedated in the Science of Sciences by Hermes. Is it not Avicenna who says that the Smaragdine Tablet — the oldest existing treatise on Alchemy — was found on the body of Hermes buried centuries ago at Hebron by Sarah the wife of Abraham? But Hermes never was the name of a man, but a generic title, just as in former times we have the Neo-Platonist, and in the present the Theosophist.

What in fact is known about Hermes Trismegistus, or

Hermes three times the greatest? Less than we know of Abraham, his wife Sarah and his concubine Agar, which St. Paul declares to be an allegory. Even in the time of Plato, Hermes was already identified with the Thoth of the Egyptians. But this word Thoth does not mean only "intelligence"; it means also "assembly" or school. In truth Thoth Hermes is simply the personification of the *voice* of the priestly caste of Egypt; that is to say of the Grand Hierophants. And if this is the case can we tell at what epoch of prehistoric times this hierarchy of initiated priests began to flourish in the land of Chemi. And even if this were possible we should still be far from having arrived at a complete solution of our problem. For ancient China, no less than ancient Egypt, claims to be the land of the alkahest and of physical and transcendental alchemy; and China may very probably be right. A missionary, an old resident of Pekin, William A. P. Martin, calls it the "cradle of alchemy." Cradle is hardly the right word perhaps, but it is certain that the celestial empire has the right to class herself amongst the very oldest schools of occult Science. In any case alchemy has penetrated into Europe from China as we shall prove.

In the meantime our reader has a choice of solutions, for another pious missionary, Hood, assures us solemnly that alchemy was born in the garden "planted in Haden on the side towards the east." If we may believe him, it is the offspring of Satan who tempted Eve in the shape of a Serpent; but the good man forgot to follow up his assertion to its legitimate conclusion as is proved even by the name of the science. For the Hebrew word for Serpent is Nahash, plural Naha-shim. Now it is from this last syllable *shim* that the words chemistry and alchemy are derived. Is this not clear as day and established in agreement with the severest rules of philology?

Let us now pass to our proofs.

The first authorities in archaic sciences — William Godwin amongst others — have shown us on incontestable evidence that, though alchemy was cultivated by nearly all the nations of antiquity long before our era, the Greeks only began to study it after the beginning of the Christian era and that it only became popularized very much later. Of course by this is meant only the lay Greeks, not of course the Initiates. For the Adepts of the Hellenic temples of Magna Grecia knew it from the days of the Argonauts. The European origin of alchemy dates therefore from this time, as is well illustrated by the allegorical story of the Golden Fleece.

Thus we need only read that which Suidas says in his lexicon with reference to this expedition of Jason, too well known to require telling here:

Deras, the Golden Fleece which Jason and the Argonauts, after a voyage on the Black Sea in Colchis, took with the aid of Medea, daughter of Metes, of Æetes, of Æa. *Only instead of taking that which the poets pretended they took, it was a treatise written on a skin which explained how gold could be made by chemical means.* Contemporaries called this skin of a ram the Golden Fleece, most probably because of the great value attaching to the instructions on it.

This explanation is clearer and much more probable

than the erudite vagaries of our modern mythologists, for we must remember that the Colchis of the Greeks is the modern Meretie of the Black Sea; that the Rion, the big river which crosses the country, is the Phasis of the Ancients, which even to this day contains traces of gold; and that the traditions of the indigenous races who live on the shores of the Black Sea, such as the Mingrelians, the Abhaziens and the Meretiens are all full of this old legend of the golden fleece. Their ancestors say they have all been "makers of gold," that is to say they possessed the secret of transmutation which in modern times we call alchemy.

In any case it is certain that the Greeks were ignorant of the hermetic science up to the time of the Neo-Platonists (*towards the end of the fourth and fifth centuries*) with the exception of the initiated, and that they knew nothing of the real alchemy of the ancient Egyptians whose secrets were certainly not revealed to the public at large. In the third century we find the Emperor Diocletian publishing his famous edict and ordering a careful search to be made in Egypt for books treating of the fabrication of gold, which were collected together and made into a public auto-da-fe. W. Godwin tells us that after this there did not remain one single work on alchemy above ground in the kingdom of the Pharaohs and for the space of two centuries it was never spoken of. He might have added that there remained underground still a large number of such works written on papyrus and buried with the mummies ten times millenarian. The whole secret lies in the power to recognize such a treatise on alchemy in what appears to be only a fairy tale, such as we have in that of the golden fleece or in the romances of the earlier Pharaohs. But it was not the secret wisdom hidden in the allegories of the papyri which introduced alchemy into Europe or the hermetic sciences. History tells us that alchemy was cultivated in China more than sixteen centuries before our era and that it had never been more flourishing than during the first centuries of Christianity. And it is towards the end of the fourth century, when the East opened its ports to the commerce of the Latin races that alchemy once again penetrated into Europe. Byzantium and Alexandria, the two principal centers of this commerce, were quickly inundated with works on the transmutation.

Let us compare the Chinese system with that which is called Hermetic Science.

1. The twofold object which both schools aim at is identical; the making of gold and the rejuvenating and prolonging of human life by means of the *menstruum universale* and *lapis philosophorum*. The third object or true meaning of the "transmutation" has been completely neglected by *Christian* adepts; for being satisfied with their belief in the immortality of the soul, the adherents of the older alchemists have never properly understood this question. Now, partly through negligence; partly through habit, it has been completely struck out of the *summum bonum* sought for by the alchemists of Christian countries. Nevertheless it is only this last of the three objects which interests the real Oriental alchemists. All initiated adepts despising gold and having a profound indifference for life, cared very little about the first two.

2. Both these schools recognize the existence of two

elixirs: the great and the small one. The use of the second on the physical plane transmutes metals and restores youth. The Great Elixir, which was only symbolically an elixir, conferred the greatest boon of all: the immortality of consciousness in the Spirit, the Nirvana which in the sequence of evolution precedes Paranirvana or absolute union with the One Essence.

3. The principles which form the basis of the two systems are also identical, that is to say: the compound nature of metals and their emanation from one common seminal germ. The letter *tsing* in the Chinese alphabet which stands for "germ," and *t'ai,* "matrix," which is found so constantly in Chinese works on alchemy, are the ancestors of the same words which we meet with so frequently in the alchemical treatise of the Hermetists.

4. Mercury and lead, mercury and sulfur are equally in use in the East and in the West, and adding to these many others we find that both schools accepted them under a triple meaning, the last or third of these being that which European alchemists do not understand.

5. The alchemists of both countries accept equally the doctrine of a cycle of transmutation during which the precious metals pass back to their basic elements.

6. Both schools of alchemy are closely allied to astrology and magic.

7. And finally they both make use of a fantastic phraseology, a fact which is noticed by the author of *Studies of*

Alchemy in China, who finds that the language of western alchemists, while so entirely different from that of all other western sciences, imitates perfectly the metaphorical jargon of eastern nations, proving that alchemy in Europe had its origin in the far East.

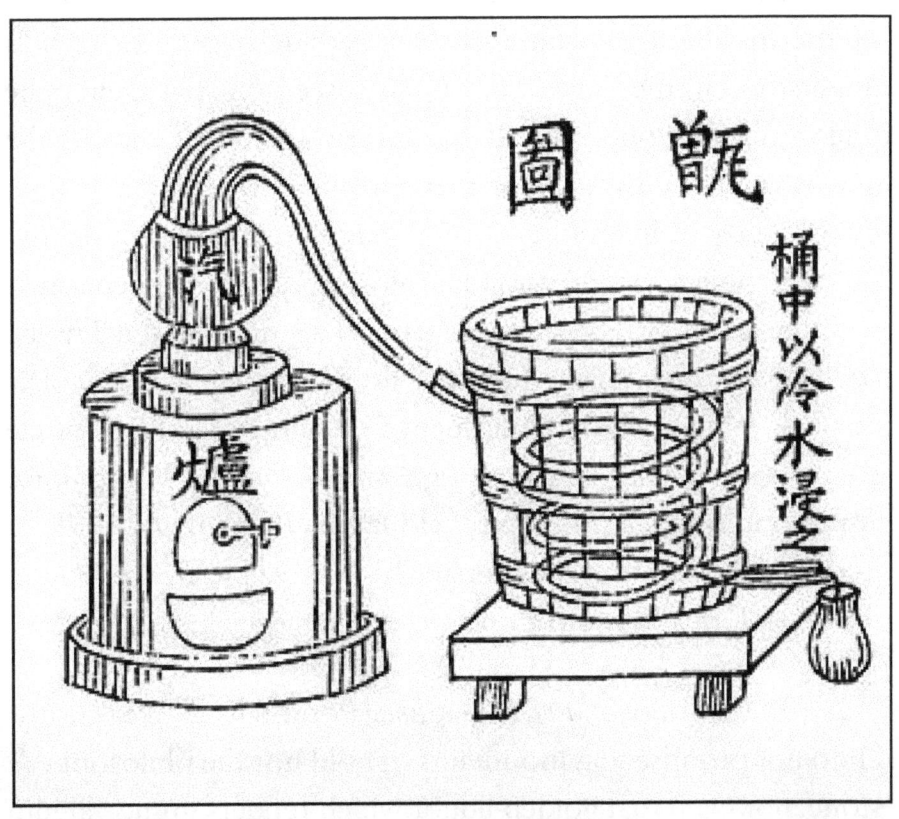

Nor should any prejudices be entertained against alchemy because we say that it is closely connected with astrology and magic. The word magic is an old Persian term which means "knowledge," and embraced the knowledge of all sciences, both physical and metaphysical, studied in those days. The wise and priestly classes of the Chaldeans taught magic, from which came magism and gnosticism. Was not Abraham called a *Chaldean?* And was it not Joseph, a pious Jew, who, speaking of the patriarch, said that he taught mathematics, or the esoteric science, in Egypt, including *the science of the stars,* a professor of magism being necessarily an astrologer?

But it would be a great mistake to confuse the alchemy of the middle ages with that of antediluvian times. As it is understood in the present day it has three principal agents: the philosopher's stone used in the transmutation of metals; the *alkahest* or the universal solvent; and the *elixir vitae* possessing the property of indefinitely prolonging human life. But neither the real philosophers nor the Initiates occupied themselves with the last two. The three alchemical agents, like the Trinity, *one and indivisible,* have become three distinct agents solely through falling under the influence of human egotism. While the sacerdotal caste, grasping and ambitious, anthropomorphized the Spiritual One by dividing it into three persons, the false mystics separated the Divine Force from a universal Kriyasakti and turned it into three agents.

In his *Magie Naturelle* Baptista Porta tells us this clearly: "I do not promise you mountains of gold nor the philosopher's stone, nor even that golden liquor which renders immortal him who drinks it. . . All that is only visionary; for the world being mutable and subject to change all that it produces must be destroyed."

Geber, the great Arabian alchemist, is even more explicit. He seems, indeed, to have written down the following words with a prophetic forecast of the future: "If we have hidden aught from thee, thou son of science, be not surprised; for we have not hidden it especially from thee, but have made use of a language which will hide the truth from the wicked in order that men who are unjust and ignoble may not understand it. But thou, son of Truth, seek and thou wilt find the gift, the most precious of all. *You, sons of folly, impiety, and profane works, cease endeavoring to penetrate the secrets of this science; for they will destroy you and will hurl you into the most profound misery.*"

Let us see what other writers have to say on the question. Having begun to think that alchemy was after all solely a philosophy entirely metaphysical instead of a physical science (*in which they erred*), they declared that the extraordinary transmutation of base metals into gold was merely a figurative expression for the transformation of man, freeing him of his hereditary evils and of his infirmities in order that he might attain to a degree of regeneration which would elevate him into a divine Being.

This in fact is the synthesis of transcendental alchemy and is its principal object; but this does not for all that represent every end, which this science has in view. Aristotle said in Alexandria that "the philosopher's stone was not a stone at all, that it is in each man, everywhere, at all times, and is called the final aim of all philosophers."

Aristotle was mistaken in his first proposition though right with regard to the second. On the physical kingdom, the secret of the Alkahest produces an ingredient which is called the philosopher's stone; but for those who care not for perishable gold, the alkahest, as Professor Wilder tells us, is only the *allgeist,* the divine spirit, which dissolves gross matter in order that the unsanctified elements may be destroyed. . . . The *elixir vitae* therefore is only the waters of life which, as Godwin says, "is a universal medicine possessing the power to rejuvenate man and to prolong life indefinitely."

Dr. Kopp, in Germany, published a *History of Chemistry* forty years ago. Speaking of alchemy, looked at especially as the forerunner of modern chemistry, the German doctor makes use of a very significant expression such as the Pythagorean and the Platonist will understand at once. "If," says he, "for the word World we substitute the microcosm represented by man, then it becomes easy to interpret."

Eirenaeus Philalethes declares that:

> *The philosopher's stone represents the whole universe (or macrocosm) and possesses all the virtues of the great system collected and compressed into the lesser system This last has a magnetic power which draws to it that which affinitises with it in the universe. It is the celestial virtue which spreads throughout creation, but which is epitomized in a miniature abridgment of itself (as man).*

Listen to what Alipile says in one of his translated works: "He who knows the microcosm cannot long remain ignorant of the macrocosm. This is why the Egyptians, those zealous investigators of nature, so often said: *Man, know thy Self."* But their disciples, more restricted in their powers of appreciation, took this adage as being allegorical and in their ignorance inscribed it in their temples. But I declare to you, whoever you may be, who desires to plunge into the depths of Nature, that if that which you seek you do not find within yourself you will never find it without. He who aspires to a first place in the ranks of Nature's students will never find a vaster or better subject of study than he himself presents.

Therefore following in this the example of the Egyptians and in agreement with the Truth which has been shown to me by experience, I repeat these very words of the Egyptians with a loud voice and from the very bottom of my soul, "Oh man, know thyself, for the treasure of treasures is entombed within you."

Eirenaeus Philalethes, cosmopolitan, an English alchemist and Hermetic philosopher, wrote in 1659 alluding to the persecution to which philosophy was subjected:

> *Many of those who are strangers to the art think that to possess it they must do such and such a thing, like many others we thought so too, but having become more careful and less ambitious of the three rewards (offered by alchemy), on account of the great peril we run we have chosen the only infallible one and the most hidden...*

And in truth the alchemists were wise so to do. For living in an age when for a slight difference of opinion on religious questions men and women were treated as heretics, placed under a ban and proscribed, and when science was stigmatized as sorcery, then it was quite natural, as Professor A. Wilder says, "that men who cultivate ideas which are out of the general line of thought should invent a symbological language and means of communication amongst themselves which should conceal their identity from those thirsting for their blood."

The author reminds us of the Hindu allegory of Krishna ordering his adopted mother to look into his mouth. She did and saw there the entire universe. This agrees exactly with the Kabbalistic teaching which holds that the microcosm is but the faithful reflection of the macrocosm — a photographic copy to him who understands. This is why Cornelius Agrippa, perhaps the most generally known of all the alchemists, says:

> *It is a created thing, the object of astonishment both to heaven and earth. It is a compound of the animal, vegetable and mineral kingdoms, it is found everywhere, though recognized by few, and is called by its real name by no one, for it is buried under numbers, signs, and enigmas without the help of which neither alchemy nor natural magic could reach perfection.*

The allusion becomes even clearer if we read a certain passage in the *Enchiridion* of Alchemists:

> *Therefore I will render visible to you in this discourse the natural condition of the philosopher's stone wrapped in its triple garment, this stone of richness and of charity, which holds all secrets and which is a divine mystery the like of which Nature in her sublimity has not in all the world. Observe well what I tell you and remember that it has a triple covering, namely: the Body, the Soul, and the Spirit.*

In other words this stone contains the secret of the

transmutation of metals, that of the elixir of long life and of *conscious immortality*.

This last secret was the one which the old philosophers chose to unravel, leaving to the lesser lights of modern times the pleasure of wearing themselves out in the attempt to solve the two first. It is the "Word" or the "infallible name," of which Moses said that there was no need to seek it in distant places "for the Word is close to you; it is in your mouth and in your heart."

Philalethes, the English alchemist, says the same thing in other terms.

> *Our writings will be like a double-edged knife for the world at large, some will use them to hew out works of art, others will only cut their fingers with them. Nevertheless it is not we who are to blame, since we warn most seriously all those who attempt the task that they are undertaking to master the most elevated philosophy in Nature. And this is so whether we write well or badly. For though we write in English, these writings will be Greek to some who will, nevertheless, persist in believing that they have well understood us, while in reality they distort in the most perverse manner that which we teach; for can it be supposed that those who are naturally fools should become wise simply by reading books which testify to their own natures?*

D'Espagnet warned his readers in the same way. He prays the lovers of Nature to read little, and then only those of whom the veracity and intelligence is above suspicion. Let the reader seize quickly a meaning which the author may probably only darkly hint at; for, he adds, truth lives in obscurity; Hermetic philosophers deceive most when they appear to write most clearly, but ever divulge more secrets, the more obscurely they write. The truth cannot be given to the public; even less in these days than in those days when the Apostles were advised not to cast pearls before swine. All these fragments, which we have just cited, are, we hold, so many proofs of that which we have advanced. Outside of the schools of Adepts, almost unapproachable for western students, there does not exist in the whole world — and more especially in Europe, one single work on Occultism, and above all on Alchemy, which is written in clear and precise language, or which offers to the public a system or a method which could be followed as in the physical sciences. All treatises, which come from an Initiate or from an Adept, ancient or modern, unable to reveal all, limit themselves to throwing light on certain problems which are allowed to be disclosed to those worthy of knowing, while remaining at the same time hidden from those who are unworthy of receiving the truth, for fear they should make a selfish use of their knowledge.

Therefore, he, who complaining of the obscurity of writers of the eastern school, should confront them with those of either the middle ages or of modern times which seem to be more clearly written, would prove only two things: first, he deceives his readers in deceiving himself; secondly, he would advertise modern charlatanism, knowing all the time that he is deceiving the public. It is very easy to find semi-modern works which are written with precision and method, but giving only the personal ideas of the writer on the subject, that is to say, of value only to those who know absolutely nothing of the true occult science. We are beginning to make much of Eliphas Levi, who alone knew probably more than all our wise men of the Europe of 1889 put together. But, when once the half-dozen books of the Abbe Louis Constant have been read, re-read and learnt by heart, how far are we advanced in practical Occultism, or even in the understanding of the theories of the Kabbalah? His style is poetical and quite charming. His paradoxes, and nearly every phrase in each of his volumes is one, are thoroughly French in character. But even if we learn them so as to repeat them by heart from the beginning to the end, what pray has he really taught us? Nothing, absolutely nothing — except, perhaps, the French language. We know several of the pupils of this great magician of modern times, English, French and German, all men of learning, of iron wills, and many of whom have sacrificed whole years to these studies. One of his disciples made him a life annuity which he paid him for upwards of ten years, besides paying him 100 francs for every letter when he was obliged to be away. This person at the end of ten years knew less of magic and of the Kabbalah than a chela of ten years standing, of an Indian astrologer.

We have in the library at Adyar his letters on magic in several volumes of manuscripts, written in French and translated into English, and we defy the admirers of Eliphas Levi to show us one single individual who would have become an Occultist even in theory, by following the teaching of the French magician.

Why is this since he evidently got his secrets from an

Initiate? Simply because he never *possessed the right to initiate others.* Those who know something of occultism will understand what we mean by this; those who are only pretenders will contradict us, and probably hate us all the more for having told such hard truths.

The secret sciences, or rather the key which alone explains the mystery of the jargon in which they are expressed, cannot be developed; like the Sphinx who dies the moment the enigma of its being is guessed by an Oedipus, they are only occult as long as they remain unknown to the uninitiated. Then again they cannot be bought or sold. A Rosicrucian *"becomes,* he is not made" says an old adage of the Hermetic philosophers, to which the Occultists add, "The science of the gods is mastered by violence; conquered it may be, but it never is to be had for the mere asking." This is exactly what the author of the Acts of the Apostles intended to convey when he wrote the answer of Peter to Simon Magus: "May thy gold perish with thee since thou hast thought that the gifts of God may be bought with money." Occult wisdom should never be used either to make money, or for the attainment of any egotistical ends, or even to minister to personal pride.

Let us go further and say at once that — except in an exceptional case where gold might be the means of saving a whole nation, even the act itself of transmutation when the only motive is the acquisition of riches, becomes black magic. So that neither the secrets of magic nor of occultism, nor of alchemy, can ever be revealed during the existence of our race, which worships the golden calf with an ever-increasing frenzy.

Therefore, of what value can those works be which promise to give us the key of initiation for either one or the other of these two sciences, which are in fact only one.

We understand perfectly such Adepts as Paracelsus and Roger Bacon. The first was one of the great harbingers of modern chemistry; the second that of physics. Roger Bacon in his "Treatise on the admirable Forces of Art and of Nature" shows this clearly. We find in it a foreshadowing of all the sciences of our day. He speaks in it of powder for cannons, and predicts the use of steam as a motive power. The hydraulic press, the diving bell, and the kaleidoscope, are all described; he prophesies the invention of flying machines, constructed in such a way that he who is seated in the middle of this mechanical contrivance, in which we easily recognize a type of the modern balloon, has only to turn a mechanism to set in motion artificial wings which begin to beat the air in imitation of those of a bird. Then he defends his brother alchemists against the accusation of using a secret cryptography.

The reason for the secrecy which is maintained by the Wise of all countries is the general contempt and indifference shown for the profounder truths of knowledge, the generality of people being unable to use those things which are of the highest good. Even those amongst them who do have an idea which proves related to something of real utility, owe it generally to chance and their good fortune; so that failing to appreciate its full meaning they fall into scientific errors to the great detriment and ruin, not only of the few, but often of the many.

All of which proves that he who divulges our secrets is worse than foolish, unless he veils that which he discloses to the multitude, and disguises it so cleverly that even the wise understand with difficulty. There are those amongst us who hide their secrets under a certain way of writing, as for example using only consonants so that he who reads this style of writing can only decipher the true meaning when they know the meaning of the words (*the hermetic jargon*). This kind of cryptography was in use amongst the Jews, the Chaldeans, the Syrians, the Arabs, and even the Greeks, and largely adopted in former times especially by the Jews. This is proved by the Hebrew manuscripts of the New Testament, the books of Moses or the Pentateuch rendered ten times more fantastic by the introduction of Masoretic points. But as with the Bible, which has been made to say everything required of it except that which it really did say, thanks to Mesorah and the fathers of the Church, so it was also with Kabbalistic and alchemical books. The key of both having been lost centuries ago in Europe, the Kabbalah (the *good* Kabbalah of the Marquis de Mirville, according to the ex-rabbi, the Chevalier Drach, the pious and most Catholic Hebrew scholar) serves now as a witness confirmatory of both the New and the Old Testaments. According to modern kabbalists, the Zohar is a book of modern prophecies, especially *relating to the Catholic dogmas of the Latin Church,* and is the fundamental stone of the Gospel; which indeed might be true if it were admitted that both in the Gospels and in the Bible, each name is symbolical and each story allegorical; just as was the case with all sacred writings preceding the Christian canon.

Before closing this article, which has already become too long, let us make a rapid *resume* of what we have said.

I do not know if our argument and copious extracts will have any effect on the generality of our readers. But I am sure, at all events, that what we have said will have the same effect on kabbalists and modern *Masters* as the waving of a red rag in front of a bull; but we have long ceased to fear the sharpest horns. These *Masters* owe all their science to the dead letter of the Kabbalah; and to the fantastic interpretation placed on it by some few mystics of the present and the last century, on which "Initiates" of libraries and museums have in their turn made variations, so that they are bound to defend them, tooth and nail. People will see only the raging fire of contest, and he who raises the greatest conflagration will remain the victor. Nevertheless — *Magna est veritas et praevalebit.*

1. It has been asserted that alchemy penetrated into Europe from China, and that falling into profane hands, alchemy (*like astrology*) is no longer the pure and divine science of the schools of Thoth-Hermes of the first Egyptian Dynasties.

2. It is also certain that the Zohar, of which both Europe and other Christian countries possess fragments, is not the same as the Zohar of Simon Ben Yochai, but a compilation of old writings and traditions collected by Moses de Leon of Cordova in the thirteenth century, who, according to Mosheim, has followed in many cases the interpretations which were given him by Christian Gnostics of Chaldea and Syria he went

to seek them. The real, old Zohar is only found whole in the Chaldean Book of Numbers, of which there only now exist two or three incomplete copies, which are in the possession of initiated rabbis.

One of these lived in Poland, in strict seclusion, and he destroyed his copy before dying in 1817; as for the other, the wisest rabbi of Palestine, he emigrated from Jaffa some few years ago.

3. Of the real hermetic books there only remains a fragment known as the "Smaragdine Tablet," of which we shall presently speak. All the works compiled on the books of Thoth have been destroyed and burnt in Egypt by the order of Diocletian in the third century of our era. All the others, including Pymander, are in their present form merely recollections, more or less vague and erroneous of different Greek or even Latin authors, who often did not hesitate to palm them off as genuine hermetic fragments. And even if by chance these exist they would be as incomprehensible to the "Masters" of today as the books of the alchemists of the middle ages. In proof of this we have quoted their own thoroughly sincere confessions. We have shown the reasons they give for this (*a*) their mysteries were too sacred to be profaned by the ignorant, being written down and explained only for the use of a few initiates; and they are also too dangerous to be trusted in the hands of those who might mistake their use; (*b*) in the middle ages the precautions taken were ten times as great; for otherwise they stood a good chance of being roasted alive to the great glory of God and His Church.

The key to the jargon of the alchemists and of the real meaning of the symbols and allegories of the Kabbalah only are now to be found in the East. Never having been rediscovered in Europe, what now serves as the guiding star to our modern kabbalists so that they shall recognize the truths in the writings of the alchemists and in the small number of treatises which, written by real initiates, are still to be found in our national libraries?

We conclude, therefore, that in rejecting aid from the only quarter from whence in this our century they may expect to find the Key to the old esotericisms and to the Wisdom religion, they, whether kabbalists, elect of God or modern Prophets, throw to the winds their only chance of studying primitive truths and profiting by them.

At all events we may be assured that it is not the Eastern School which loses by the default.

We have permitted ourselves to say that many French kabbalists have often expressed the opinion that the Eastern school could never be worth much, no matter how it may pride itself on possessing secrets unknown to Europeans *because it admits women into its ranks.*

To this we might answer by repeating the fable told by brother Jos. N. Nutt, Grand Master of the Masonic lodges of the United States for women, to show what women would do if they were not shackled by males — whether as men or as god.

A lion passing close by a monument representing an athletic and powerful figure of a man tearing the jaws of a lion said: "If the scene which this represents had been executed by a lion the two figures would have changed places." The same remark holds good for Woman. If only she were allowed to represent the phases of human life she would distribute the parts in reverse order. She it was who first took Man to the Tree of Knowledge, and made him know Good and Evil; and if she had been let alone and allowed to do that which she wished, she would have led him to the Tree of Life and thus rendered him immortal.

www.ingramcontent.com/pod-product-compliance
Lightning Source LLC
LaVergne TN
LVHW041502070426
835507LV00009B/765